Contents

Words appearing in the text in bold, **like this**, are explained in the Glossary.

 Find out more about what it's like to use a wheelchair at www.heinemannexplore.co.uk

Who uses a wheelchair?

Children and adults use a wheelchair if they have difficulty walking. Some people use their wheelchair all the time. Sometimes another person helps them by pushing the wheelchair.

Using a Wheelchair

Angela Royston

Heinemann

www.heinemann.co.uk/library

Visit our website to find out more information about **Heinemann Library** books.

To order:

☎ Phone 44 (0) 1865 888066

🖹 Send a fax to 44 (0) 1865 314091

💻 Visit the Heinemann Bookshop at www.heinemann.co.uk/library to browse our catalogue and order online.

First published in Great Britain by Heinemann Library, Halley Court, Jordan Hill, Oxford OX2 8EJ, part of Harcourt Education.
Heinemann is a registered trademark of Harcourt Education Ltd.

Editorial: Sarah Shannon and Richard Woodham
Design: Ron Kamen, Victoria Bevan and Celia Jones
Picture Research: Maria Joannou and Kay Altwegg
Production: Amanda Meaden

Originated by Dot Gradations Ltd
Printed and bound in China by South China Printing Company

10 digit ISBN 0 431 11224 X (hardback)
13 digit ISBN 978 0 431 11224 4 (hardback)
09 08 07 06 05
10 9 8 7 6 5 4 3 2 1

10 digit ISBN 0 431 11230 4 (paperback)
13 digit ISBN 978 0 431 11230 5 (paperback)
10 09 08 07 06
10 9 8 7 6 5 4 3 2 1

British Library Cataloguing in Publication Data
Royston, Angela
  Using a wheelchair– (What's it like?)
  362.4'383

A full catalogue record for this book is available from the British Library.

Acknowledgements
The publishers would like to thank the following for permission to reproduce photographs:
Action Plus p.**24** (Glyn Kirk); Alamy pp.**8** (Dennis MacDonald), **10** (Sally & Richard Greenhill), **15** (Photo Network), **17** (Pixel shepherd), **22** (Photofusion Picture Library), **26** (Image100), **27** (Popperfoto); Corbis pp.**11** (Harcourt Index), **20** (Colin Garratt/Milepost 92); Getty Images/Imagebank pp.**4** (Gary S & Vivien Chapman); Getty Images/Stone p.**9** (Don Smetzer); PA Photos p.**5** (DPA Deutsche Press-Agentur); Photodisc pp.**12** (Getty), **21** (Getty), **28** (Getty); Rex Features p.**19** (Phanie); Science Photo Library pp.**6** (John Greim), **29** (Lee Powers); Tudor Photography pp.**7, 13, 14, 16, 18, 23, 25**.

Cover photograph of a boy in a wheelchair, with friends, reproduced with permission of Imagestate.

Every effort has been made to contact copyright holders of any material reproduced in this book. Any omissions will be rectified in subsequent printings if notice is given to the publishers.

The paper used to print this book comes from sustainable resources.

A wheelchair can be used in many different places.

Some people can only walk short distances. They use their wheelchair for long distances, such as getting around at school or going shopping.

Why are wheelchairs used?

To be able to walk, your body needs to do many different things at once. Your **bones** and **muscles** must be strong, and your **brain** needs to tell your muscles what to do.

Some elderly people can find it hard to walk long distances.

This man can use his hands to open a packet of tissues, but cannot use his legs to walk.

Some **injuries** and illnesses can make a person's bones and muscles too weak to carry them. Other injuries and illnesses mean the brain cannot tell the muscles what to do.

How can you help?

When you meet someone in a wheelchair, treat them as you would like to be treated yourself. If someone is pushing the chair, do not talk to them about the person in the chair.

Do not lean on a wheelchair or hang on to it.

Someone in a wheelchair might not always need help or want it. Always ask the person first before trying to help.

Types of wheelchair

Powered wheelchairs allow people to get around outside easily. They have motors and are controlled by buttons and **levers** on the **armrest**.

Powered wheelchairs make it easy to get around.

Some wheelchairs fold up so they can be stored in the **boot** of a car. Sports wheelchairs are made so that they can turn, stop, and start quickly.

This wheelchair is designed for speed!

Using a wheelchair

People need strong arms to use a wheelchair by themselves. They turn the back wheels to move around. They **brake** by stopping the wheels with their hands.

Getting up and down steps is the hardest thing to do in a wheelchair. The person using the wheelchair must **balance** using the back wheels while lifting the front wheels on to the step.

Everyday life at home

People in wheelchairs can do many things that other people do. Provided they can reach, they can stack a dishwasher, load a washing machine, and use an oven to cook.

A washing machine can be used from a wheelchair.

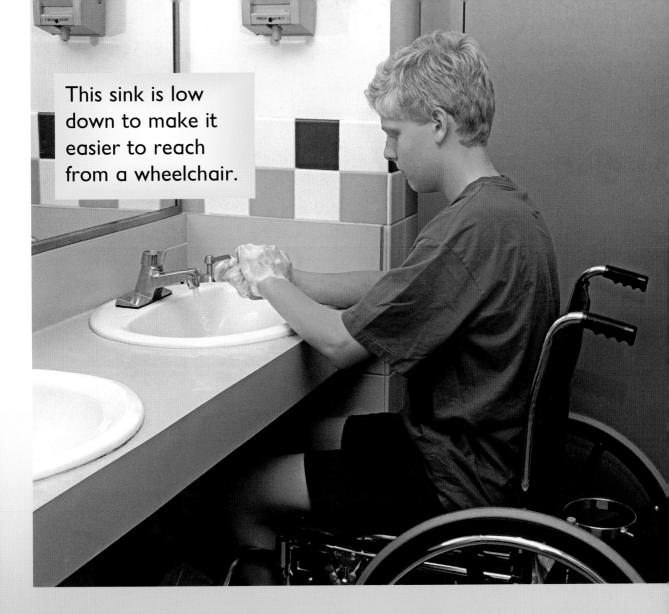

This sink is low down to make it easier to reach from a wheelchair.

Making small changes to everyday objects can help people who use wheelchairs. Handles on a bath can help someone to get in and out.

Help at home

Remote controls make televisions and other electrical machines easier to use. You can even get remote controls for light switches, windows, and doors.

Without a stairlift, this person would not be able to climb the stairs.

People who live in homes with stairs may need a **stairlift**. The lift is fitted to the side of the stairs and can carry a person up and down the stairs.

Getting about

Getting about outside can be hard in a wheelchair. Doors and passages have to be wide enough for a wheelchair.

Automatic doors are good because they open for you!

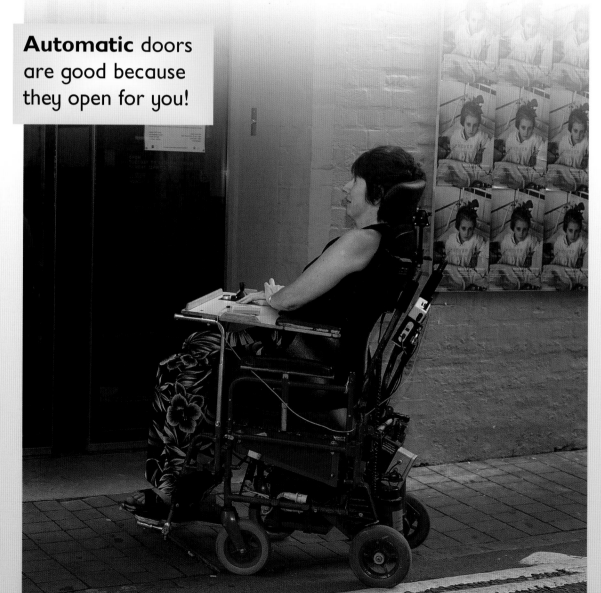

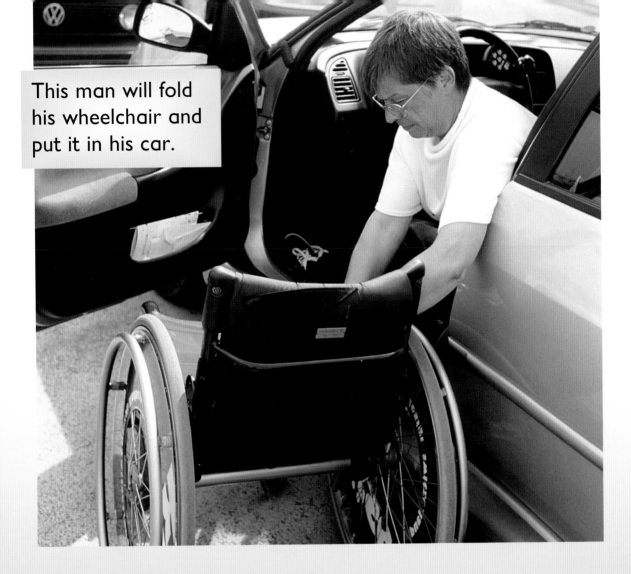

This man will fold his wheelchair and put it in his car.

Many people who use wheelchairs also drive their own cars. The controls are all worked by hand. Many car parks have some spaces set aside for cars driven by people who use wheelchairs.

Travelling

Travelling by **public transport** can be hard with a wheelchair. Railway stations and airports have special **ramps** and lifts, but the **staff** must put them in place every time they are needed.

This woman will help the man in the wheelchair get on to the train.

Platforms like this one can be found on many buses.

Some buses have special lifts for people using wheelchairs. A **platform** slides out and slowly drops down. It then lifts the chair on to the bus.

Going up!

Steps and stairs are a problem for people in wheelchairs. Buildings such as **libraries**, **hospitals**, and **museums** often have long **ramps** as well as steps.

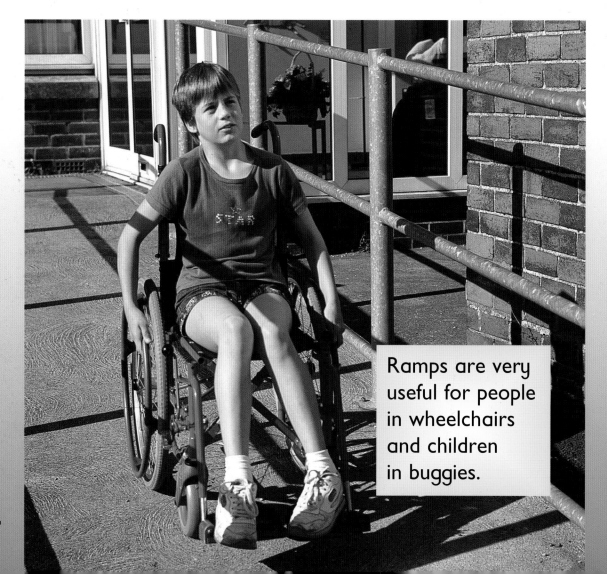

Ramps are very useful for people in wheelchairs and children in buggies.

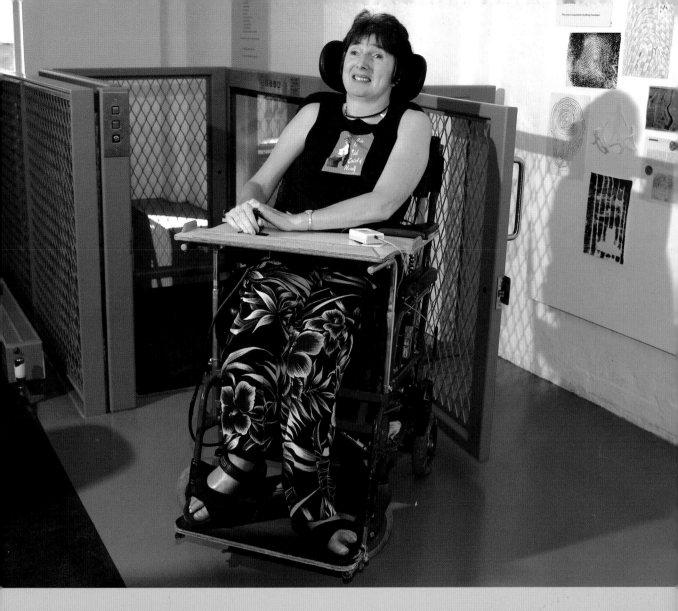

Large buildings, such as blocks of flats and offices, usually have lifts. A lift is the only way that someone in a wheelchair can reach the higher floors.

Going out

People in wheelchairs enjoy the same things as everyone else. Sports grounds and theatres often have a space at the front for people in wheelchairs to watch from.

Some **restaurants** have tables with enough space between the table legs for wheelchairs. Tables that have one support in the middle give the most space for wheelchairs.

Sport

Many people in wheelchairs play sports, such as basketball, swimming, and snooker. Some people cannot walk but they can play rugby or hang-glide!

Wheelchair basketball is a popular game to watch or play.

Some wheelchair users race in **marathons**. Others take part in the Olympics for people with a disability, called the Paralympics.

Wheelchair racing is fast and exciting.

School and work

Being in a wheelchair should not stop people from learning or working. New schools and **universities** are built with **ramps** and lifts as well as stairs.

This man's wheelchair fits easily under his desk.

Many jobs can be done by a person in a wheelchair. People in wheelchairs are often very good at solving problems and dealing with **challenges**.

Find out more

Wheelchairnet
Lots of facts and advice about using wheelchairs. Go to 'Town Hall' for frequently asked questions.
www.wheelchairnet.org

Whizz-Kidz
The Kidz Zone is a great website where you can swap messages with people who use wheelchairs and read about famous people who use them.
whizz-kidz.atticmedia.com

British Wheelchair Sports Foundation
This is where to go if you want to get involved in wheelchair sports such as basketball.
www.bwsf.org.uk

Association of Wheelchair Children
Go to 'What we do' and 'Case studies' to read about how using a wheelchair has changed the lives of other people.
www.wheelchairchildren.org.uk

 Find out more about what it's like to use a wheelchair at www.heinemannexplore.co.uk

Glossary

armrest part of a chair that supports your arm

automatic works by itself

balance remain upright

bones hard parts inside your body that give your body its shape

boot space at the back or front of a car for storing things

brain part of the body that controls the rest of the body

brake slow down or stop moving

challenge something that is hard for you to do

hospital place where sick or injured people are treated

injury damage to a part of the body

lever stick used to make something move

library place where books are kept for people to read or borrow

marathon race of just over 26 miles (42 kilometres)

motor machine that uses electricity or fuel to make something move

muscles parts of the body that give it the power to move

museum place where rare, valuable, and interesting things are kept and shown to the public

platform raised flat area

powered driven by a motor

public transport bus, train, tram, or aeroplane that anyone can travel on after buying a ticket

ramp slope connecting a lower level to a higher level

remote control object that allows you to control something, such as a television, from a distance

restaurant place where you can buy and eat a meal

stairlift small lift that carries a person up and down the stairs

staff group of people who work at a particular place

university place where people can go to continue learning after they have left school

---

More books to read

Labanowich, Stan, *Wheelchair Sports: Wheelchair Basketball* (Capstone Press, 1998)

Powell, Jillian, *Sam Uses a Wheelchair* (Evans Brothers, 2004)

31

Index